Abanindranath Tagore (1871-1951)was born in Jorasanko, Kolkata. He is the nephew of the poet and Nobel Laureate Rabindranath Tagore. Though he is primarily acclaimed as a painter and was one of the principal supporters of oriental art, his fame as a writer was no less. In fact he painted both with his brush and words. *Rajkahini, Buro Angla, Khirer Putul, Nalak* are some of his famous literary works.

Abanindranath Tagore's

KHIRER PUTUL

The Doll of Condensed Milk

Translated by
AMITA RAY

HAWAKAL PUBLISHERS

Published by: **Hawakal Publishers**, 185, Kali
Temple Road, Nimta, Calcutta 700049, India.

Website: www.hawakal.com
Contact: info@hawakal.com

First edition: May, 2018

Printed and bound at *S. P. Communications,*
Kolkata

Copyright © 2018 Amita Ray

Cover concept and illustrations: Jayanta Biswas

ISBN-13: 978-93-87883-06-2
Price: INR 250/- [USD 9.00]

RAKA
My six- month-old little angel

Foreword

Abanindranath Tagore (1871- 1951) was a young man of around twenty-five years when he published Khirer Putul in 1896. Abanindranath, nephew of the poet and Nobel laureate Rabindranath Tagore, distinguished himself as a painter on canvas as well as a painter of word-pictures. The latter were children's narratives which were exquisitely written and illustrated. So Abanindranath Tagore's magical word play, lucid and sparkling with the use of clusters of vivid images became the hallmark of his books for children such as *Rajkahini*, *Nalak*, *Buro Angla* and of course *Khirer Putul*. Abanindranath Tagore's creative work carried the signature imprint of originality and creative freedom, these skills being integral attributes of the illustrious Tagore family. There was a time when urban and suburban, educated and cultured families in undivided colonial Bengal, governed by the British Raj, had regaled the new generations of children born into their families with readings from the books of Abanindranath Tagore along with the poems for children written by his uncle Rabindranath Tagore.

Interestingly, in his Introduction to Dakshinaranjan Mitra Majumdar's *Thakurmar Jhuli* first published in 1907, eleven years after the publication of Abanindranath Tagore's *Khirer Putul* (1896), Rabindranath Tagore had written, "Is there anything more Swadeshi than *Thakurmar Jhuli, (The Grandmother's Bag)*? But alas, in recent times, even this bag full of sweets has come already manufactured from the factories of Manchester. Nowadays, fairy tales from the West have become almost the sole recourse of our boys. The Grandmother Companies from our own country are bankrupt. If one rustles their bags, perhaps a copy of Martin's *Ethics* or Burke's notebooks on the French Revolution might pop out–but where are our princesses, our magic birds–*Byangoma* and *Byangomi* or the gem of seven kings that lies beyond seven seas and thirteen oceans" [1]

Tagore's regret and caveat was scripted in 1907. Now in 2018, in independent India, more than

---

[1]Maitra, Lopamudra. *100 years of Thakurmar Jhuli (Grandmother's Bag of Tales): From Oral Literature to Digital Media– Shaping Thoughts for the Young and Old . citeseerx.ist.psu.edu.*

a century later this regret lingers even today, as there seems to be a far greater propensity towards reading of the British *Harry Potter* series with all its fantasy creatures, instead of the rich vernacular resources which are no less enchanting and engrossing for readers both young and old. Alas, cultural colonization is more deep rooted than political colonization of the state.

The use of a global language along with a local language, that is the use of the English language as well as a vernacular language for communication and academic purposes, continued simultaneously, even after India's independence and perhaps up to the 1990s, despite the burgeoning of English medium schools that used English as the first language for instruction. Now, quite often we notice that Bengali in West Bengal has been reduced to a spoken language. Young school-going children are unable to read and write in Bengali as the parents and English medium schools both prefer to develop the skills of the children in the official Indian language, Hindi, rather than in the state language, Bengali.

So post-'90s, that is in the last few decades, with the advent of globalization, we find children in West Bengal are often sadly ignorant of Bengali children's literature written by Rabindranath Tagore, Abanindranath Tagore, Upendrakishore Roy Choudhuri, SukumarRoy, Lila Majumdar among many others.

As a result, we are now both aggrieved and aware about the onset of what one can describe as cultural globalization, leading to local cultures being systematically appropriated, distorted or destroyed. As a result, a homogeneous culture generated by the media and elite educational institutions is eroding the vibrant heterogeneity of India's diverse local cultures and the many rich languages that have produced outstanding creative literature. Though Bangladesh, due to its troubled historical past and political sensitization, has been successful to a remarkable extent to protect and preserve Bengali literature and language from the onslaught of the global lingua franca English. West Bengal has not been able to resist the hegemonic thrust of linguistic imperialism.

Therefore, the nurturing institutions of young minds, the families and schools, now slowly but steadily regard local cultures and languages as exotic, ethnic and essentialist, consequently, these are now peripheral to one's basic formal educational qualifications and sense of identity as an achiever. Ethnic clothes are regarded by native young people as fancy dresses for ethnic celebrations. Similarly skills in vernacular language and literature are no longer considered primary objectives but optional achievements

that are invariably not considered priorities.

In such an environment, one way of preserving the regional languages and regional literature that are being devoured by the ubiquitous English language, is to use English translations to sustain local cultures and practices, as children and youth of the present are seen to shy away from developing skills in reading, studying and writing vernacular texts.

Amita Ray's translation into English of Abanindranath Tagore's timeless Bangla original text *Khirer Putul*, does just that. In her sensitive and skilful translation, Amita Ray has been able to replicate the swift-flowing lucidity and charm of the original Bangla text by Abanindranath Tagore. The success of a translated text of creative writing is its readability. This is undoubtedly the acid test. Amita Ray's translation of *Khirer Putul* has passed this test with flying colours. Those children and their parents among others, both at home and in the world, that is, specifically those who are unable to read the Bengali language, will be immensely grateful to the translator for enabling them to read *Khirer Putul* in English translation.

Also, it is interesting how *Khirer Putul* can be read not just as a children's fantasy tale about a king, two queens and a very clever "black-faced monkey". As a cultural critic I would like to read the narrative as a delightfully transgressive text where the Goddess Shashti is being fooled and forced into succumbing to the clever ploys of a monkey, who soon enough proves himself as a skilled strategist. The monkey fools the king too as well as all the people in the kingdom. He tells everyone that the King's senior wife, *Duorani*, would bear him a son soon.

The overtly patriarchal text also underscores that kings could have several wives and polygamy was common. Eventually the narrative concludes as the son-producing elderly wife, *Duorani*, is felicitated as the reigning Queen of the kingdom. The beautiful, barren and jealous young wife, *Suorani*, who was initially the King's favourite queen, could not bear the cruel neglect of the king who became besotted with his son-bearing senior wife, *Duorani*. As the tale concludes, the young, beautiful but barren *Suorani*, dies of heartbreak.

In 1907 when Dakhinarajan Mitra Majumdar published *Thakurmar Jhuli* (*The Grandmother's Bag*) readers noticed that as in *Khirer Putul*, here too were the two contesting queens, *Suorani* and *Duorani*. The intense desire of not just the king but the people of the kingdom was that the Queen had to produce male heirs. Also, it must be noticed that the hero of Abanindranath

Tagore's *Khirer Putul* is not any male human agency, not even a prince in the disguise of a monkey, but an ever agile and cerebral monkey who even tricks a Goddess, apart from seamlessly tricking the king almost all throughout the engrossing tale.

In fact, when the young beautiful Queen *Suorani* asked the King to bring jewellery and clothes for her as gifts, when he was going on a journey, the senior Queen *Duorani*, who lived in a hovel outside the palace asked for a monkey-"The queen said, "I feel ashamed to ask for ornaments. Bring if you must, a black faced monkey." Could this be Abanindranath Tagore's ironic deconstruction of the legendary notions of women's desires for material embellishments? Could this be a satirical comment on male wisdom for the narrative unequivocally reposes heroic attributes and empathy to a black-faced monkey, who emerges as the hero of *Khirer Putul*.

As admitted by Abanindranath Tagore, the source narrative of *Khirer Putul* was an unpublished fairy tale in Rabindranath Tagore's wife Mrinalini Devi's draft collection of fairy tales and fantasies. Incidentally, Mrinalini Devi was the aunt of Abanindranath Tagore. Abanindranath Tagore hadstated without ambiguity that Mrinalini Devi's unpublished draft was the source text of *Khirer Putul*,"it is from her exercise book that I borrowed the idea of my story, *Khirer Putul*." [2]

As the source story was written or collected or transcreated by a married woman and a mother, Mrinalini Devi, a member of the elite Tagore family, it is riveting to notice the gendered binaries between the good and suffering wife and the evil and greedy wife, the child-bearing wife and the barren wife, as epitomized in the roles of *Suorani* and *Duorani*. *Khirer Putul* therefore can be read from a gendered perspective, as the narrative overtly consolidates gender stereotypes.

I hope this competent translation of Abanindranath Tagore's *Khirer Putul* by Amita Ray, who was my classmate at the Postgraduate Department of English, Calcutta University, will be read by lay readers of translated texts along with researchers engaged in gender studies, translation studies, comparative folk literature studies and children's literature studies.

Sanjukta Dasgupta
March 27, 2018

[1] Abanindra Rachanavali Volume 1, page 370. Kolkata : Prakash Bhavan

Introduction

Khirer Putul, written by Abanindranath Tagore, is an enchanting Bengali fairytale and an eternal favorite among young readers. In my childhood I was so captivated by the charm of this story that I read and re-read it innumerable times without ever getting tired of it. So when translating children's literature crossed my mind, this book, my childhood obsession became the instantaneous choice. Not only is it a hearty read for the target audience, the not so young and those young at heart find it fascinating too.

Khirer Putul is a fairy tale inspired by the traditional Bengali folk lore and folk culture. The tapestry of the tale is woven with a preponderance of mythical allusions, rituals, imageries, nursery rhymes and allegories; a repertoire derived from the storehouse of Bengali folk culture and traditions. It is replete with fantasy episodes, the flavour of which is steeped in local customs, conventions and cultural connotation. Capturing every nuance of the original text proved a bit tricky at times but it was negotiated without undermining the innate rhythm and essence of the masterpiece. Some words which were best left as they appear in the source text have been appended at the end of this story to facilitate smooth reading.

Translating *Khirer Putul* was an engaging experience as childhood memories of my fondness for the book became alive during the process. I remain forever grateful to *Sanjukta Dasgupta* for her generous suggestions and sincere help whenever I happened to knock her. I thank the entire team of *Hawakal Publishers* for being supportive from the very day I approached them till the last.

Once upon a time there lived a king. He had two wives— Duorani and Suorani. Suorani was excessively pampered and lived a lavish life in the royal palace. Seven hundred maids looked after her, washed her feet, tinged them with *aalta* and styled her coiffure. Seven basket-full of flowers were brought from seven gardens with which Suorani made garlands. Jewels and ornaments as vast as that of seven kingdoms taken together filled her chests. She adorned herself with these ornaments. The king could die for her!

Duorani, the elder of the two queens was totally uncared for. The king detested her. He had given her a dilapidated cottage to live in, a deaf and dumb maid to be at her service. She had   a tattered bedspread to sleep on and a faded sari to wear. The king came to Duorani's room just once in a year, sat for a moment, uttered a word or two and departed.

It was in Suorani, the younger queen's room in the palace where the king stayed the entire year.

One day the king called his minister and said, "Well, I wish to travel to countries far and wide. You get the ships ready."

At his bidding, the minister started to prepare the ships for the voyage. It took seven months to get seven ships ready for the ensuing voyage. Six ships would carry the king's attendants and retinue, while the king himself would set sail in a ship made of gold, shaded with gilded canopy.

The minister came and informed, "Your majesty, everything is ready for the voyage."

The king said, "We will start tomorrow". The minister departed.

The king went to take leave of his beloved queen Suorani who was relaxing on her golden cot. Seven maids were at her beck and call. Sitting on the cot beside his dear queen the king indulgently asked, "I will set sail for distant lands tomorrow. What shall I bring for you my love?"

Toying with the diamond bangles on her delicate wrist, she chirped, "Diamonds look extremely pale and they don't beautify my hands. How I love to wear eight bangles of ruby as red as blood if I could get them."

The king assured her to get eight bangles of ruby from the land of rubies.

Playfully dangling her fair feet and jingling her anklets she again cooed, "These anklets do not tinkle well. I wish to wear a string of ten fiery -red anklets made of gold if I get."

The king agreed saying, "From the land of gold I shall get for you the anklets."

Pointing at the pearl necklace she had on her the queen complained, "Your Highness, these pearls are too small. I have heard about pearls in a distant country which are as large as the pigeon's eggs. Get me a necklace made of those pearls."

The king said, "The land of pearls is located in the ocean. I shall fetch a pearl necklace from there. What more do you wish for my dear queen?"

Then the much pampered queen wrapped her sari's end around her beautiful body and whined, "My God! This is more of a burden than a *sari*! I wish to feel comfortable in a sari as blue as the sky, feathery as the wind and light as water."

Consoling her, the king said, "Alas, it's so dear. The golden sari has bruised your golden body, causing pain to your skin as tender as butter. Dear queen, do bid me good bye with your sweet smile so that I can bring for you a *sari* as blue as the sky, feathery as the wind and light as water."

The queen bid him good bye with a bewitching smile.

As the king was about to leave the palace and set out on his voyage, it suddenly struck him that he hadn't met his miserable Duorani.

Duorani, the elder consort was lying on her torn coverlet and weeping when the king entered her humble cottage. Standing by the door of her ramshackle shelter, the king said, "Oh queen, I am about to set out on a voyage to foreign lands. I will bring Suorani bangles for her hands, necklace for her neck, anklets for her feet and sari to drape on. What shall I bring for you? Tell me what you wish for."

The queen replied, "Oh king, all my wishes will be fulfilled if you return home safe and sound. When I was your beloved queen I had many a wishes. I would then long to be seated amidst thousands of maids draped in a golden sari. I would wish to tie golden anklets in the feet of *Shuk shari* birds kept in golden cage. I craved for many things of which many have been fulfilled. What purpose will golden ornaments and golden *sari* serve now? Your Highness, for whose love shall I adorn myself with diamond bangles and pearl necklace? For whose delight should I tie ornament of precious stones on my head? Alas, those days are no more!

You may give me golden ornaments, but I will never get back your love! You will never return me those seven hundred maids together with the palace of   seven mansions! You may bring me a bird from the forest but my king; you won't give me a golden cage! I will lose my gold ornaments to thieves and dacoits from this humble dwelling of mine and the bird from wilderness will not remain in a broken cage. Oh king! You may take leave from me now and fulfill the desire of the queen you love at present. Who cares for my wishes?"

The king pleaded, "No my queen, it can't be so. People will speak ill of me. Do tell me what you want."

The queen said, "I feel ashamed to ask for ornaments. Bring if you must, a black faced monkey."

The king replied, "Okay, my queen, allow me to take leave of you."

Then   Duorani burdened with grief, collapsed on her ragged coverlet and bade the king farewell with tears in her eyes. The king departed and embarked the ship.

In the evening the golden ship with wind in its golden mast set out like a golden cloud in the blue water towards the west.

Fixing her gaze in that direction Duorani lay on the worn out coverlet of her humble cottage. The king's love Suorani, in her royal palace with seven hundred companions to wait upon her was lulled to sleep upon her golden cot by the song of a golden bird, dreaming of her cherished ornaments.

Once on the ship the king also forgot about his grief stricken queen Duorani. Thinking of the happy face of Suorani on the parting day he mused, "What is my queen doing now? Probably she is doing her hair. What's she up to now? Must be putting *aalta* on her feet. Maybe now she is plucking flowers from the seven gardens, wonder if she is making garlands now and thinking about me! With me in mind she probably is shedding tears and is unable to make garlands. Most likely the golden threads, flowers in the basket are lying at her feet. She must be spending sleepless nights being absorbed in my thoughts."

Suorani, the younger queen, the beloved of the king was always in his thoughts. The elder queen Duorani was crazy for the king's love but the king didn't think of her for once.

Thus the king spent twelve months journeying in his ship far and wide. On the thirteenth month the king's ship reached the land of rubies.

In the land of rubies everything starting from the walls of houses, steps leading to the ponds and gravels on roads were made of rubies. From that land of rubies, the king got Suorani's ruby bangles crafted. Eight thousand rubies were used for eight bangles which when worn would look like blood spilling out of the skin.

With the ruby bangles the king went to the land of gold. Over there the king got ten strings of anklets made of pure gold crafted by the goldsmith. The anklets glittered like sparks of fire, and chimed like the sweet sound of *veena*.

The king with ruby bangles from the land of rubies, golden anklets from the land of gold finally arrived in the land of pearls.

In the king's garden of the land of pearls there are two pigeons. The birds have pearl feet, ruby beaks, eat pearl fruits from emerald trees and lay eggs of pearl. The queen of that land makes garland with those pearls in the evening, dons it on her coiffure and discards it the next morning.

Her maids sell those used pearls in the market for a shipful of silver.

The king bought a string of pearl for Suorani with a shipful of silver.

Then with the ruby bangles, golden anklets crafted from the land of gold and pearl necklace strung from the land of pearls in his possession, the king sailed and reached yet another country after six months. In the wilderness of that country belonging to the princess, on sapphire trees with sapphire leaves there are blue silk worms which feed on the leaves of sapphire, spin sky-blue-coloured threads of silk as fine as water and ethereal as the breeze. Then the princess sitting on the terrace the whole night weaves a blue silk *sari* matching its shade with that of the sky above. It takes her six months to weave the sari. Only once does she wear that sari the color of which is as blue as the sky, breezy as the wind and light as water. She then drapes herself in the sari, visits the temple of *Lord Shiva* and worships him. Returning home, the princess takes off her sari, the maids sell the sari to anyone who can afford seven shipful of gold. The king bought such a sari which his beloved Suorani had pined for with seven ships of gold.

Then voyaging for another six months on seven oceans and thirteen rivers the king with his seven ships reached homeland with the queen's ruby bangles, golden anklets, pearl necklace and her much cherished sari. Then suddenly he remembered that the elder queen had asked for a monkey. The king said to the minister, "I have made a great mistake. I haven't brought a monkey for my elder queen. Go and search for one."

The minister went off to look for a monkey while the king riding a white elephant made way through the crowded road of his kingdom. With the ornaments and sari he went straight to the room of the palace where Suorani lived.

Suorani at that time was on the seventh floor of her palace of seven mansions, combing her hair seated in front of a golden mirror. Parting her hair with a golden comb the queen had done her hair with golden laces and pins and was applying vermilion between her eyebrows. Taking *Kajal* from the *kajal* case she darkened her eyes, embellished her feet with *aalta*. The maids were waiting upon her with platters of beetle leaves and flowers. At that moment the king entered her chamber.

Sitting beside the queen on the crystal throne the king said, "Look here my dear queen, from the land of rubies where everything is made of rubies I have brought these ruby bangles for you. These are the gold anklets from the golden land of gold sand and dust. In the land of pearls two birds having legs of pearl and beaks of ruby lay pearl eggs. The queen of that land strings those pearls in a garland, adorns her bun with it and disposes of it the next morning. Beloved, I have brought one of them for you. In a certain kingdom the princess spins seven strands of thread from a single silk thread. Then sitting on the terrace at night spins one sari which takes her six months. She then wears it for a day, goes to offer prayers and on returning home discards it. Dear queen I have brought such a sari for you at the cost of seven shipful of gold. Take a look at these gifts and put them on as I have travelled far and wide to get them for you."

The queen then wore the ruby bangles but they were too big in size and reached up to her shoulders. Next the queen wore the anklets on her feet. Alas! They were too loose, slid down her rosy ankle and dropped on the floor before she had hardly taken two steps. Disgruntled, the queen put on the pearl string but it was so short in length that it bruised the flesh of her neck. The queen was in pain!

The queen next draped on the *sari* she had wished for; the blue sari woven with blue silk strands turned out to be short in length. Tears welled up in her eyes.

The queen was so hurt that she took off her ruby bangles made of eight thousand rubies, pushed away the anklets with her feet; discarded the pearl necklace and the sari which she had pined for. Then she cried out, "Fie my lord!

What worthless ornaments! What a useless sari! The bangles are made of the gravels of which country? The anklets are crafted of sand and dust of which country? Fie! The pearl string is made from left over pearls of someone! The *sari* is a worn and throwaway piece of which princess! The very sight of these stuff is disdainful, to wear them a shame! Oh king! Take them away. I have nothing to do with a worn sari and used ornaments."

The queen was so upset that she went to a room and locked herself to sulk in seclusion. Crestfallen, the king departed to his royal court with the discarded ornaments and sari bought for a hefty price.

The minister was sitting on one side of the king's throne with a young monkey which he had bought from a merchant's ship in a magician's land. He bought it for a paltry sum after going through the fields, riverside and market places of the kingdom.

Seeing him the king said, "Oh minister, I am amazed! I had brought ornaments of right measurement and a sari for my younger queen but they didn't fit her!

Then that monkey from the forest, touching the feet of the king said, "Unless one is very fortunate and virtuous, the *sari* woven by a nymph and necklace crafted by a mystical serpent princess cannot be worn. You must keep them in the royal treasury and give them to your future daughter in law to be worn."

The king was surprised at the monkey's words. On a merry note he asked his minister, "What does the monkey say? Having no son, how do I bring in a daughter in law? Well, go to the goldsmith and place an order of new ornaments for my younger queen, go to the weaver and ask him to weave a new *sari* for her. Keep these ornaments and sari away in the royal treasury as gifts for my daughter in law in case I happen to welcome one to my house."

Off the minister went to the goldsmith for new ornaments to be crafted and the king went to the elder queen with the monkey in his arms.

The miserable elder queen wiped the king's feet with the end of her worn out sari and asked him to sit on the ragged coverlet in her ramshackle cottage. She sobbed and said, "My king, do sit on this frayed coverlet in my humble abode. What else do I have to offer you to sit down? Alas my lord, you have returned after such a long time and so unfortunate am I to lay this tattered coverlet for you to sit on.

On hearing these words the king was moved to tears. He sat on the tattered bedspread and

placing the baby monkey on the queen's lap said, "My dear queen, your tattered bedspread and ramshackle cottage are a thousand times better than the younger queen's golden throne and gilded chamber. There is love, care and loving words in this humble cottage, things which are absent there. I had brought for her golden ornaments and *sari* for seven shipful of gold but she has spurned them. I have brought for you just a monkey costing a worthless coin and you have lovingly accepted it. My queen, I will never bring sorrow to you. Allow me to take leave now but I will come again. Take care to see that the younger queen doesn't know about it! If she comes to know that I have paid you a visit then her wrath will descend upon us! She will either kill you or me by giving poison."

Thus consoling the elder queen, the king departed. The elder queen started to bring up the monkey with milk and banana in her humble cottage.

The days passed by. The younger queen spent her days in the palace amidst seven hundred maids while the elder queen spent hers in the dilapidated cottage, bringing up the baby monkey on the worn out coverlet. Day after day, month after month and year after year elapsed. The elder queen's unhappiness remained undiminished with coarse rice for meals, *sari* made of rough thread to wear. In that gloomy cottage the elder queen with her sole companion of sorrow, the monkey from wilderness on her lap would gaze at the younger queen's palace of seven mansions, seven gardens, shedding tears.

Whenever the monkey caught sight of the queen he would find her eyes moist with tears. Not for a single day did he see her smile!

One day the monkey asked, "Well mother, why do you always cry? What is your grief? What makes you cry looking at the palace? Who stays there?"

The queen replied, "Everything that is mine is there. I have a palace of seven mansions, seven hundred maids, seven chests of ornaments and seven flower gardens. My dear, in that palace I have a *sateen* who is now the king's younger wife. That giantess has cast a spell on my king, forcibly taken possession of him and my palace along with the seven hundred maids, seven chests of ornaments and all that is mine. She lives happily in that golden palace surrounded by flower gardens. She has snatched away the crowning glory of all my wealth, my king and turned me into a street beggar. My dear son, what should I be sorry for! At first I was the daughter of a king and then became the wife of a monarch, seven hundred maids were at my beck and call, lived in that beautiful palace and above all got a royal husband I had dreamt of. I was blessed with everything I could wish for but know not by whose evil curse I could not give birth to a lovely prince for my king! Alas! I must have committed sins in my previous births, hindered others from fulfilling their wishes, inflicted sorrow in the heart of many a mother. As a result of my misdoings during this birth I have to pay the price by handing over my loving family to my *sateen*, forgo my pride as queen, be deprived of the love of my king as well as the hope of giving birth to a prince and embrace the life of a beggar! My dear, a stone hearted creature as I am still live on having endured such insult and pain so long!

Narrating her woeful story, the queen's bosom flooded as tears trickled down her eyes. Then the monkey from the woods rested on the queen's lap and wiping away her tears consoled, 'Mother, don't you cry. I will drive away all your sorrow, will restore you your palace of seven mansions surrounded with seven flower gardens, seven hundred maids and in the golden temple you will be seated beside the king with a darling son on your lap. Only then, will I be rightfully entitled to the name of a monkey. If you can do as I say then you will again reign in your palace with your past glory and grandeur."

Hearing the words of the monkey tears of joy glistened at the corner of the queen's eyes, a smile wafted on her lips. Laughing and crying in unison the queen said, "Dear son, I have made many sacrifices in temples and offered prayers while on many a pilgrimage but have not been blessed with a son. What austerities would you observe, by dint of the blessing of which god would you, a mere monkey from the woods restore me to my rightful place as the queen with a prince on my lap? Leave it my dear, may my king live in happiness, my *sateen* too live in joy; let me be content with my burden of woes. You need not worry about making the impossible possible. It's quite late at night, go to sleep."

The monkey insisted, "No mother I won't sleep unless you listen to me."

The queen said, "No dear, it's getting quite late at night. Go to sleep! Clouds have gathered in the east and west, it is raining heavily, the kingdom now is in deep slumber. So you too go to bed dear. Tomorrow I shall listen to anything you say, but today you should sleep. I have shut the door of my humble cottage as a storm is raging outside. I have spread the coverlet on the floor as it is cold. My sweet little child, come, come close to my bosom and sleep on my lap."

Resting his head on the queen's bosom, the monkey fell asleep while the queen placed her head on the worn out bedspread and fell asleep too.

Thus the night passed. The younger queen spent the night on her golden cot bedecked with flowers along with the king while the elder queen lay on her torn bedspread in the decrepit cottage with the gale and rain raging outside.

Then the day dawned. The hours chimed from the guard's room of the palace and the royal couple woke up to the note of *sehenai*. The king washed his face with crystal clear water poured from a golden pitcher, put on his royal garments and descended to his royal court. The younger queen in her flower decked golden bed turned aside and again fell asleep in the soothing breeze of floral hand fan.

And what did the elder queen do?

The queen woke up to the golden sun rays which entered her humble cottage. She looked in every direction but could not spot her monkey. The queen looked for him from one room to another, searched in the thatched roof of her cottage, even on the branches of trees. The monkey was nowhere in sight! The elder queen started to cry

Where had the monkey disappeared?

The monkey had left for the royal court before the day dawned leaving the sleeping queen to herself.

The king was seated in his royal court surrounded by ministers and courtiers, with royal sentry guarding the entrance and people thronging around. The queen's monkey making his way through the crowd slipped in escaping the attention of the guards and soldiers, touched the feet of the king and declared, " Your majesty, I have good tidings for you! My mother will give birth to a son."

The king asked, "Is it true? Duorani, the elder queen will bear me a son? Well, if this news proves false both you and your mother Duorani will be beheaded.

The monkey replied, "Your Majesty it's my worry. Now make me happy and I shall take leave of you."

The king took off the string of elephant pearls he wore on his neck and offered it to the monkey as a parting gift. Dancing in glee, the monkey reached the tumbledown cottage of Duorani where she lay crying bitterly.

Wiping away the queen's tears and dust the monkey said, "Look here mother, see what I have brought for you! You being the royal queen do not even get a necklace to put on, instead of it you buy a wooden neck string and wear it; now I have this pearl string for you to wear!"

Looking at the elephant pearl neckpiece the monkey was holding the queen asked, "Where did you get this? This is the pearl string the king wears on his neck I had made this when I was the queen. Where on earth did you get this? Speak out monkey; did the king throw away this pearl string? Did you pick it up from the royal road?"

The monkey replied, "No mother, I didn't pick it up from anywhere. How can a string of elephant pearls, which you yourself have threaded and worn by the king, be picked up from the road?"

The queen asked, "Did you then steal it from the king's room?"

The monkey exclaimed, "What a shame mother, should anyone steal! Today I gave the king good news; so the king has pleased me by gifting me this pearl necklace.

The queen said, "Oh my darling, you are the son of a miserable mother, a monkey from the wilderness. What good tidings for the king made you run away to the palace before dawn from the lap of your distressed mother who resides in this ramshackle cottage!

The monkey replied, "Mother I dreamt that a brother of mine was born, a son was born to you and that son has ascended the throne as king. So I rushed to the king to give the news that a son will be born to my mother. The king became so happy that taking off the pearl necklace from his neck he offered it to me as a reward."

The queen said, "My dear boy, today the king has heard what you have said and believed it. But tomorrow he will find out that it is false news. Today he has rewarded you with a pearl necklace; tomorrow he will command his men to behead us. Alas! What have you done? I get little to eat and live with; at least I am fortunate enough to see the king once a year. Oh, you have ruined everything! Why have you spread this rumor? Why have you brought about this disaster?"

The monkey replied, "Why are you afraid and disturbed? Just keep quiet for these ten months. Let everyone know that a child will be born to the elder queen. Then when the time comes for the king to see his son, I will give a beautiful son on your lap to be shown to the king. Come now, it's getting late and I am feeling hungry."

The queen said, "Come my dear, I have kept a bowl full of water and brought fruits from the trees for you to eat."

The queen sat on a broken low wooden stool to feed the monkey.

And the king went to the younger queen.

The younger queen had woken up from a nightmare and sat on the golden cot thinking about it. Just then the king entered the chamber and informed her, "Have you heard that the elder queen will give birth to a child! I was very much worried with the thought of who would succeed me to the throne and now I am free from such worries! If the child is a boy, he will ascend the throne and if it's a daughter I will marry her off and give my kingdom to my son in law. Dear queen, I was in deep anxiety but at last am relieved of it."

The queen retorted, "Oh, I can't stand it anymore— I am fed up with the troubles you create for me and to think of those of others!"

Astonished, the king chided, "What are you saying my queen? Can such words be uttered on such a happy day? How can one make a long face on hearing that a prince will be born who will one day be crowned the king? My queen, everyone in the palace is happy with the news, then why do you wish evil?"

The queen said, "This is unbearable! I certainly can't worry about things like whose son will be crowned the king, whose daughter will inherit the kingdom, who will ascend the throne. I have my own burden of woes to worry about, I have nothing to do with the son of others and do not care whether they live or die. Oh my god! My morning sleep is disturbed with such foolish talk and my head is aching. Let me go and have my bath."

The vexed queen, jingling her eight bangles and ten strings of anklets went away from the other side.

The king grew furious. The younger queen had wished the prince death! The dejected king retired to the outer mansion of the palace. The king and queen quarrelled. He stopped seeing the face of the younger queen. He didn't also visit the elder queen lest the younger queen poisons the elder queen to death on hearing it! The king stayed all alone in the outer mansion of the palace.

Month after month elapsed but the king and queen remained estranged. They quarrelled for four months at a stretch. On the fifth month the tamed monkey of the elder queen, Duorani met the king. The king asked, "Well now monkey, what news?"

The monkey replied, "Your Majesty, my mother is in deep sorrow. The coarse rice she eats is unpalatable; she stays without eating and has become feeble."

The king said, "Well, I am not aware of this fact. Minister, go immediately and get the finest quality rice, and fifty dishes to be served in golden plates and bowls and send them to the elder queen. From today, the elder queen will have all the dishes that I am served with. Go minister, give the monkey a hundred gold coins and bid him good bye."

The minister took leave of the monkey and hurried to the kitchen. The queen's monkey went to his mother with a bagful of gold coins.

The queen asked, "Now, where have you been today?" It's quite late in the day and I have not been able to take my bath. When shall I cook and when shall we eat?"

The monkey consoled, "Well mother dear, you don't have to cook anymore. The finest quality rice together with fifty dishes on golden plates will arrive for you from the palace. So take your bath quickly."

The queen went away to take her bath. The monkey went to the market with a handful of gold coins. With sixteen of the gold coins he hired sixteen people who make thatched cottages, bought sixteen cartful of hay and

sixteen hundred bamboos. With those sixteen hundred bamboos, sixteen carts full of hay and employing those sixteen hundred men, the monkey reconstructed Duorani's ramshackle cottage in the wink of an eye. New bed sheet of patchwork was spread in the bedroom, new low wooden stools kept in the dining room and sixteen cooks brought lunch for the queen from the palace kitchen. The monkey offered them sixteen gold coins before they left!

Taking her bath Duorani returned to her cottage. She found her cottage transformed into a new one. The thatched roof was new! The bedspread on the floor was new! The sari on the dress-stand was new too! The queen was astonished. She asked the monkey, "Well dear, I set out from a dilapidated cottage to have my bath. How come I find it absolutely new on returning?"

The monkey said, "Mother dear, the king offered me gold coins with which I have transformed your dilapidated cottage into a new one, spread new coverlet and laid new wooden stools. Come and have warm rice from golden plate and drink warm milk from golden bowl."

The queen sat down to have her food. After a long time she ate from a golden plate, washed her mouth with water poured from a golden container, had beetle leaves from a golden platter; still she was not contended. Eating her royal meal she mused, "Today the king has sent fine rice on a golden plate, but tomorrow he might behead me in the heath."

Thus the queen spent months in anxiety. The new cottage became old, holes reappeared in the thatched roof, and the hay of the roof flew away. The monkey went to meet the king.

The king asked, "Well monkey, what brings you here?"

The monkey answered, "Your Majesty, should I utter in fear or without fear?"

The king said, "Speak without fear."

The monkey said, "Your majesty, my mother lives in misery in her dilapidated cottage. The door of the cottage is broken, there is no hay on the thatch, and cold wind enters her room. My mother doesn't have quilt to cover herself, no wood to light a fire, the whole night she shivers in cold."

The king asked, "So is it! You should have told me this earlier! Bring your mother to the royal palace and I will get it arranged for her to stay."

The monkey replied, "Your Majesty, I am afraid of bringing my mother to the palace. The younger queen will poison her."

The king said, "You need not be afraid of that. I will keep the queen in a newly built mansion around which a moat will be dug, guards will be appointed at the entrance. The younger queen will not be able to reach her. The elder queen will stay in that mansion with her deaf and dumb nurse and you her pet son."

The monkey said, "Your Majesty, allow me to go and bring my mother."

The king ordered his minister, "Go and get the mansion ready for the queen."

The minister employed *lakhs* and *lakhs* of people and had the palace ready and decorated in a day.

Leaving her ramshackle cottage, ragged coverlet and draped in sari of gold threads, Duorani entered the new mansion. She relaxed on a golden cot, had her food served on golden plate, distributed money to the poor and needy. The whole kingdom wished glory to the queen; the younger queen flared up in anger.

The younger queen had an old *Brahmini* witch whom she lovingly nicknamed '*Heart's Secret*' as her close companion. The younger queen sent her a message to appear before her as she had something to share with her.

Hearing that the younger queen had summoned her, the old witch instantly went there.

The queen welcoming her said, "Come dear, how are you my Heart's Secret? Come, sit close to me."

Sitting next to the younger queen the *brahmini* witch asked, "Well dear, what makes you call me? Why are you sulking with tears in the corners of your eyes? What's the matter?

The queen replied, "Everything is upset! My *sateen* is back in her place. She has draped a *sari* made of golden threads, has got a new mansion to live in and has become the beloved queen of the king. That beggar of a queen Duorani has now become the royal queen and reigns in this palace! My friend, how I envy her! Give me some poison that I can end my life. I simply can't bear her being pampered!

The *brahmin* witch said, "What a shame my friend. Don't you ever utter such words! For what sorrow will you take poison? Today Duorani may have become the queen; tomorrow she will again become a beggar. You will remain the pampered Suorani of the king forever."

Suorani said, "No dear, I have no wish to live. Duorani will give birth to a son soon and that son will rule the kingdom! People will then glorify Duorani as their royal mother and say, just look at her, the blackface Suorani who couldn't gift a son to the king though she is the king's favorite! What a shame! It is ominous to even cast a glance at the face of such an ill fated person; to just utter her name brings misfortune also! Such cursed words of the people will be simply unbearable. Get for me some poison, either I have it or make my sateen have it."

Mildly chiding the queen the old *brahmini* said, "Hush my dear queen, someone might overhear us. Why do you worry? I will get for you poison secretly, you make Duorani have it. Now allow me to take leave of you so that I may go in search of poison."

The queen said, "Well, you may go now but take care to see that the poison is strong enough to have instant effect on the elder queen."

Comforting her, the old witch said, "Don't fret dear! Tomorrow when the elder queen will be made to take the poison, her wish to become the royal mother will remain unfulfilled forever. Just remain undaunted."

The witch departed to look for the poison. The whole day long she searched through the forests and at dusk spotted a snake resting in the bushes. She cast a magic spell on it and extracted deadly poison from its fangs.

The younger queen mixed that poison in a variety of sweetmeats like *muger nadu, kheerer chhach, motichoor* which she herself prepared. Arranging them on a plate she told the witch, "Well dear, do something for me. Go and sell these sweetmeats to the elder queen."

Plate in hand, the witch went to the new mansion of the elder queen. The elder queen affectionately welcomed her and said, "Come dear, where have you been so long? Should you forget me since I am Duorani?

The witch replied, "Oh, why do you say so! I live on your kindness. How can I forget you? Look here, I have taken care to bring for you sweetmeats like *muger nadu, khirer chhach* and *motichur.*"

The queen noticed that the old *brahmini* had brought sweets carefully arranged on a platter. Gladly she received them and sent her off with two fistfuls of golden coins. The old witch went away in glee.

The queen tasted a bit of the *kheerer chhach,* her tongue became numb. On consuming the *muger nadu,* her throat turned dry. On tasting *motichur,* her chest burned within. Summoning the monkey she cried, "Oh! What has the *brahmani* made me eat! I am feeling unwell, it seems I am about to die!"

The monkey suggested, "Come mother, lie down on the cot. You will get well."

The queen stood up, the snake's venom reached up to her head. The queen lost herself in darkness which appeared before her eyes, she felt dizzy and the beautiful queen collapsed on the floor.

Placing the queen's head on his lap, the monkey felt her pulse, examined her eyes by raising her eyelids. The queen lay unconscious, numb!

The elder queen as beautiful as golden idol was laid on the golden cot and the monkey ran to the forest in search of medicine. From the forest, he collected some herbs and roots, made a paste of them in the mortar and started administering it to the queen.

News arrived at the royal palace that the elder queen had taken poison. The king hurried to the queen's mansion. The royal minister followed close on the heels. The royal physician came along chanting the sacred text. Next, starting from the queen's maids, royal courtiers, servants, everyone followed suit.

The monkey asked, "Your Highness, why have you brought so many people? I have given medicine to my mother. She is doing well, let her sleep a while. Ask all the people to leave this place."

The king got the poisonous sweetmeats examined by the royal physician and asked him to leave. He gave the responsibility of the kingdom to the royal minister and asked him to leave too. The king himself stayed back in the queen's mansion.

The elder queen remained unconscious for three days and three nights at a stretch. On the fourth day she regained consciousness. She opened her eyes.

The monkey came and informed the king, "Your Majesty, the elder queen has recovered. You have been blessed with a son who is destined to be the sovereign."

The king took off his diamond necklace and offering it to the monkey said, "Come monkey, let's go and visit the queen and her son."

The monkey said, "According to astrological calculations, if you see your son's face now you will become blind. Once the son gets married you can see him. Now come and meet the elder

queen and see what distress has been inflicted on her by the younger queen."

The king saw that the reaction of the poison had transformed the golden lustre of the queen into black soot. She was lying like a snipped off leaf, the queen could no longer be recognized.

The king returned to his palace and flung the younger queen in the prison. The old witch had her head tonsured and whey poured on her. Then she was made to sit on a donkey facing hind side and thrown out of the kingdom.

Then he ordered, "Minister, today is a very auspicious day, I have been blessed with a son who is destined to be the sovereign. Go and illuminate the streets, let fireworks be burnt in all houses, open up the treasury for the poor and ailing, let there be no beggars in my kingdom."

At the behest of the king the minister lit up the streets with lights, there was a display of fireworks in all houses of the kingdom, the royal treasury was opened up for the weak and the destitute, the king was profusely praised in the kingdom.

Thus ten years passed by amidst celebrations, offering prayers at the temple and making sacrifices at the feet of Goddess *Kali*.

Then one day the king called the monkey and said, "Ten years have passed. Now let me see my son.

The monkey replied, "Your royal Highness, first of all select a wife for your son, get him married and then see your son's face. If you look at him now you will turn blind."

In compliance with the monkey's words, the king sent messengers to countries far and wide. Marriage alliances with many a princess came but the king did not find anyone suitable enough for his son.

Eventually, the messenger from Patali kingdom arrived with the picture of an exquisite looking princess enclosed in a golden casket! The complexion of the princess was akin to pure gold, she had arched eyebrows over a pair of long drawn eyes, smiling lips, tresses which when let down tumbled up to her feet. The king chose this princess as the bride.

Summoning the monkey the king said, "I have chosen my son's bride. Tomorrow is an auspicious day. In an auspicious hour I will get my son wedded to her"

The monkey said, "Your royal Highness, tomorrow in the evening send the bridegroom's palanquin along with bearers at the door of my mother. All of us will accompany the bridegroom to the wedding ceremony."

The king said, "Look here dear, for ten long years I have obeyed you and have not seen my son. If you do not allow me to see his face tomorrow all hell will be let loose."

The monkey said, "Your Highness need not worry about it. Now you leave for the palace of the father in law of your son. Tomorrow we will accompany the bridegroom to his palace."

The king hastened to the house of his son's father in law so that his glance did not fall on his son resulting in his blindness.

The monkey went to the elder queen in the new mansion.

From the moment the queen had heard of the news of her son's marriage, the queen had started crying and brooding, "Where do I get a son? What do I feign so that the king is tricked?"

The monkey came up to his mother and said, "Mother dear, do get up! Send for the bridal attire and *topor*, mould for me a little boy with condensed milk. I will dress it up as a bridegroom and get it married."

The queen said, "Dear one, don't you have fear in your heart? How do you venture to dress

up a doll made of condensed milk as a bridegroom and get it married? How do you intend deceiving the king? Leave it dear, I have feigned to become the beloved queen of the king, for that sin I have been given poison by my sateen. It's my good fortune that I have survived, how can I dare to deceive the king again? Let this entire episode end here dear. Why do you add to your burden of sins! Call the king; I will lay bare everything that has happened in front of him."

The monkey said, "Where do I get the king? It takes two days to go to the bride's place and the king has set off to her house. So without talking, make for me a bridegroom with condensed milk. The king is awaiting the bridegroom's arrival; if the bridegroom fails to reach there it will be a great insult to him. Mother dear don't worry, you send the doll of condensed milk to get married—if goddess *Sasthi* is pleased, you will be blessed with one of her sons."

Reposing faith on the monkey's words, the queen mustered enough courage to make the figure of a boy with condensed milk as her fancy would wish. She then dressed it up in bridegroom's attire, placed a golden *topor* on his head and put shoes made of golden thread on its little feet.

The monkey surreptitiously placed the bridegroom made of condensed milk on the palanquin and kept it out of sight by drawing a colorful screen on the doorway. Only two little feet of the bridegroom clad in embroidered shoes, jutting out, could be seen.

Seventeen bearers lifted up the bridegroom's palanquin on their shoulders. The monkey with turban on his head and scarf wrapped round his waist set out to get the doll of condensed milk married amidst the sound of drum beats, fluttering ensigns and dazzling lights.. The queen sat in her gloomy mansion all alone, praying fervently to the god who removes all distress and danger.

Meanwhile the bridegroom borne by sixteen bearers, torchbearers with torches, drummers with drums, the bridegroom's companions on horseback reached the kingdom of Dignagar travelling the whole night long amidst notes of flutes being played and splendour of lights.

They reached by the lake of Dignagar at daybreak. The torches had extinguished, the horses were exhausted, the bearers were tired carrying the palanquin, and the hands of the drummers had been seized with cramps by nonstop playing of drums.

The monkey ordered that tents should be put up by the lake. Asking the bearers to place the bridegroom's palanquin near a banyan tree where an idol of goddess *Sasthi* was lodged and worshipped, he asked them to leave the place. Then he called the minister and said, "It's the king's order that no one should see the bridegroom today as it would prove to be inauspicious."

The minister enforced the king's order. The king's people bathed in the lake, cooked, had their meal and lay down in the tents without venturing towards the banyan tree. When the women folks of the village came to worship goddess *Sasthi* under the banyan tree the royal guards drove them away.

Therefore goddess *Sasthi* was not worshipped that day. The goddess became restless with pangs of hunger; her throat got parched with thirst. The monkey chuckled to himself.

Thus it became quite late in the day. Goddess *Sasthi* did not receive even a drop of water to drink as she was not worshipped. The goddess became impatient within the framework of the idol; her pet black cat started whining. The monkey then hit upon an idea, he left the palanquin door open and he kept himself out of sight.

Goddess *Sasthi* mused, "Good riddance!"

Emerging from inside the framework of the idol in the scorching heat she started searching for banana and the like, offerings of worship. While looking for eatables she spied the doll of condensed milk inside the palanquin. Unable to resist her temptation, she summoned the *aunts of sleep* in her mind.

It was day in Dignagar, but in the realm of sleep it was night. The *aunts of sleep* had blessed the children of goddess *Sasthi* with nightlong sleep the previous night. In the morning they had put to sleep the princess of their realm and had just closed their eyes for a nap when they were summoned by goddess *Sasthi*. The aunts in the land of sleep woke up and they left for the kingdom of Dignagar immediately. Touching the feet of the goddess they asked, "Why have you called us mother at daytime?"

The goddess replied, "Well dears, it's quite late in the day and I haven't yet received any offerings from worship. You help me out by putting to sleep all the people in this kingdom so that I can go and devour the doll of condensed milk inside the palanquin without anyone noticing me."

The *aunts of sleep* took pity on goddess *Sasthi* and all the people in the kingdom of Dignagar were put to sleep. The shepherd in the midst of the field, the baby in its home, the mother of the baby lying beside it, the elder sibling of the baby in the playroom; all slumbered in their respective places. The king's men by the banyan tree and the children attending schools all fell asleep. The king's minister dozed off with his pipe of the *hookah* in his mouth; the head of the village dozed off cane in hand. Night descended upon Dignagar during the day. The *aunts of sleep* induced sleep in everyone's eyes. The only ones to stay awake were the stray dogs and jackals, the elephants and horses of the king's men by the lake, the birds of the forest and of course, the queen's monkey perched on top of the tree. Some others to keep awake were a variety of cats—jungle cats, water cats, tree cats and domestic cats. The goddess then opened the door of the palanquin and took the boy of condensed milk in her hand. Allured by the aroma of condensed milk, the tree cat came down from the tree, the forest cat scuttered from the forest, the water cat emerged from the water, the shy cat left its hideout and came to the banyan tree where goddess *Sasthi* was located.

Goddess *Sasthi* gave the ten fingers of the doll of condensed milk to the cats to eat. She herself fed upon the hands, legs, chest, back and head of the doll. Offering the two ears of the doll to the two aunts she asked them to depart.

The aunts went away from the realm of sleep in Dignagar. All the people sleeping near the lake woke up, the inhabitants of the village also woke from their slumber. Wiping her mouth goddess *Sasthi* was about to enter the framework of the idol when down leapt the monkey from the tree and exclaimed, "Where are you running away! First of all return the doll of condensed milk. You have been caught red-handed devouring the stolen condensed milk. I will spread a word about this scandal far and wide."

The goddess got frightened and shouted, "Get to hell! What does this black faced monkey say! Move away; let me flee before people see me!"

The monkey said, "It won't be so, first you should return the boy and only then will you be released. Else, I will immerse you along with your idol in the waters of the lake. It will be a fit enough punishment for a goddess who steals condensed milk."

The goddess felt deeply ashamed; quivering in anger she said, "Hush my dear, you may be heard. I have eaten your boy of condensed milk, how can I get him back? Yonder below the banyan tree my sons are playing. Choose a boy from among them and get him married. By my boon, the elder queen will treat him as his own. Do release me now."

The monkey said, "I cannot spot any boy under the banyan tree! Where are they? If you grant me divine vision, I can see the children of goddess Sasthi!" The goddess then stroked the monkey's eyes and he attained divine eyesight.

A whole realm of children under the banyan tree opened up in the monkey's vision; children inside houses, outside houses, on land and water, on roads and lanes, on branches of trees, over the green grass—they were present everywhere, groups of boys and girls. Some were dark complexioned, some beautiful, some dusky. Some wore anklets on their feet; some had waist bands while some wore chains of gold balls on their neck. Some were playing the flute, some jingling rattles while some were dancing and prancing about rotating their tiny hands, the anklets ringing along. Some had red shoes on their feet; some wore colorful caps, while some draped flower embroidered scarves worth a *lakh* of rupees. Some boys were thin, some well rounded, some mischievous and some quiet. While a group of boys were riding wooden horses some were fishing in the lake, some were bathing in the water of the embankment, some were gathering flowers scattered under trees and some plucking fruits from the boughs of trees. There was an ambiance of childish playfulness, joy and quarrels all around. It was indeed a new country, a dreamland. Children were running about and playing; there were no schools, no teachers of schools, no cane in the hand of the teacher. All around there was dark water of the lake, the forest of reeds flanking it, the endless stretch of fields, orchards of mangoes and jackfruits, long tailed parrots perched on trees, round eyed catfish in the river water and swarms of mosquitoes in the aurum groves. Moreover, near the forest lived the *Forest Aunties* who prepared sweet delicacies with puffed rice and on the pomegranate tree beside the house the lord of forests danced! There stood a jubilee tree by the river which bore fruits; blue horses grazed in the meadows, golden peacocks from the land of *Gour* reveled on the streets. The boys riding those blue horses decorated with golden peacocks, with Puturani in a palanquin were headed towards Kamalapuri to get her married, drums and *mridang* being played all along. It was the land of parrots, abounding with flocks of them, pecking at paddy grains sitting on perch and screeching from trees while playing with the children of that land. The people ploughed their fields with oxen, brushed their teeth with diamonds. It turned out to be an absolutely different country; in the wink of an eye morning dawned and in another wink it became evening, such was the wonder! There was sparkling water amidst dry grains of sand, a group of boys had arrived there on palanquins for fishing counting *koree*; bones of fish had pricked some tender feet while the sun shone on some beautiful visage! The son of a fisherman covering himself with fishing net was fast asleep. It was just then that it started raining pitter patter, there was a tide in the river; right then the group of boys leaving their wooden palanquins scampered away to the shelter of houses. On their way home, the fishes they had caught were snatched away by the kites, frogs pulled off their fishing rods, the boys returned home furious, their mother cooled some warm milk and gave them to drink. And beside the sand bank with glistening water, Lord *Shiva* anchored his boat, three daughters accompanied him—one daughter cooked and served, the other daughter got her fill while the third daughter angry at being deprived of her share departed to her father's house. The monkey also went to the land of her father's house along with that daughter. There he found young girls bathing on the bank of the lake; some were drying their dark tresses. On both sides of the banks two fishes *ruhi* and *katla* floated up, one of them was taken by *guruthakur* while the other was lifted by a parrot perched on a boat. On seeing this an otter holding a parrot in one hand and clasping a fish in the other started prancing. A mother sitting at the doorway of her house playfully rocking her child said, "Oh otter dear, look back to see my little boy dancing"

The monkey saw that the little boy was as handsome as the golden moon. He hastily snatched away the little boy from its mother. Instantly the visionary land before him vanished, the long tailed parrots flew away to some unknown destination in the green horizon, the boat of lord *Shiva* drifted away elsewhere. The dames bathing on the bank of the lake draping their striped saris went away. The tamed cat in the fantasy land of goddess *Sasthi* who was escorting Puturani seated in a palanquin carried by four bearers and accompanied by four maid servants to her in law's place through orchards of mangoes and jackfruits, also carrying sweetened parched paddy to win the heart of Puturani's mother in law suddenly disappeared in the darkness of the mango grove. The weasels prancing on tamarind trees receded from view, the entire land of visions seemed to get buried underground.

The monkey was amazed to find him all by himself under the banyan tree with the little boy in his arms. Where was goddess *Sasthi?* Where were the others? None was in sight! The monkey then called all the people, placed that beautiful boy on the palanquin and towards the evening left for Dignagar with lighted torches and amidst drumbeats.

Meanwhile in the kingdom of Patali, the king sitting in his son in law's palace wondered, "why hasn't the monkey turned up yet? Has he tricked me? I will behead him once I return to my kingdom."The bride mused, "I wonder how the bridegroom looks!" The bride's parents thought, "Alas! Our beloved daughter will become someone else's wife and leave us for another home." The maids and attendants of the palace thought about finishing their household chores in time so that they could go up to the terrace to see the bridegroom. Just about that time, the monkey appeared with the bridegroom amidst the sound of drums beating, bellowing of trumpets, clattering of the hooves of horses and dazzling illumination. Holding the hand of the little boy, the king welcomed him and made him sit in the wedding court; the bride's father gave her daughter's hand by marriage to the son in law.   All the neighbors welcomed the bridegroom, the maids and servants blew the conch and made the auspicious sound of *ulu*; the bride and bridegroom were thus married.

The day after marriage the king accompanied by his daughter in law, son and monkey returned to his homeland amidst pageantry and splendor. The palace of Patali became forlorn in one night; the dear daughter of the royal couple had left for her in-law's place.

In the meantime, the elder queen of the king had cried ceaselessly for the past two days and two nights in anxiety and towards the morning had drifted into sleep. In her sleep she dreamt that goddess *Sasthi* was telling her, "Get up Oh queen, look— your darling son has come home." The queen woke up and sat on her bed. At the door she could hear her attendants calling, "Wake up oh queen wake up! Wear your silk *sari* and welcome home your son and daughter in law."

The queen draped her silk *sari* and came out. There she saw that her king had really brought her son and daughter in law! Smiling she took both of them on her lap. As a result of the boon of goddess *Sasthi* she completely forgot about the boy of condensed milk during her wretched times. She thought that worrying too much about her son had made her dream about the son of condensed milk.

The king gifted his kingdom to his son and appointed the monkey as the minister of his kingdom. He blessed his daughter in law with the eight bangles studded with eight thousand rubies and adorned her feet with ten strings of golden anklets. The ruby bangles in her wrist gave the look of blood spilling out; the anklets kept jingling on her feet, glittering brightly.

Jealousy got the better of the younger queen and she died of heartbreak.

Word notes

Saree: a length of fabric usually draped by women in the Indian subcontinent.

Anchal: the end of a saree which usually hangs from the shoulder after being draped.

Sukh-shaari: fantasy birds of Bengali folk tales which can sing sweetly.

Sinthi: an ornament donned by Indian women in the central parting of hair.

Aalta: a liquid red colour used by women to adorn the borders of their feet.

Veena: a traditional Indian stringed instrument.

Shiva: one of the three main Gods of Hinduism figuring in Hindu mythology and folk lore.

Kajal: khol, an eye make-up made out of black soot used usually in the Indian subcontinent.

Sateen: co-wife.

Shehanai: an Indian wind instrument played mainly in auspicious occasions.

Lakh: a unit, in the Indian numbering system, which is equal to one-hundred-thousand.

Brahmani: a woman belonging to the higher caste Hindu in India.

Mooger nadu: a popular Indian sweetmeat made of moog beans.

Kheerer chach: sweets made by shaping condensed milk in moulds.

Motichur: sweets made out of tiny globules of fried gram flour.

Kaali: the Hindu mother goddess worshipped as the embodiment of divine energy.

Topor: a traditional headgear worn by the Bengali bridegroom.

Sasthi: the Hindu folk goddess worshipped as the benefactress of children. Her blessings are required for child bearing and the wellbeing of children.

Aunts of sleep: in folklore they refer to the maternal and paternal aunts (*mashi*, *pishi*) of sleep who bestows sleep to children.

Kheer: condensed milk.

Forest aunties: fantasy characters who stay in forests and give beautiful gifts to children.

Mridanga: a drum used in Indian music.

Koree: the outer shell of a type of sea shell which was used as money in ancient India.

Rui: a species of fish in the carp family found in rivers of South Asia.

Katla: a freshwater fish of the carp family in South Asia.

Hookah: an instrument for smoking tobacco.

Guruthakur: a preceptor, teacher.

Ulu: a high pitched sound made with the tongue by women as a ritual during auspicious occasions.